# TIGER
# AND
# BELL

BY

## DONNA WEBERNICK

# TIGER
# AND
# BELL

## BY
## DONNA WEBERNICK

ALL GRAPHICS WERE
TAKEN FROM CANVA AND MADE INTO
MY DESIGN

Dear Reader,

I hope you enjoy my children's book. My five cats inspired me to write this book.
Thank you for purchasing Tiger and Bell.

Best Regards,

Donna Webernick

A mouse lived in the attic of an old country house. One day, a family moved in.

The mouse noticed a large cat and worried that it might want to eat him.

As the Waller family moved boxes and furniture, their cat Tiger roamed the house, searching for a scent.

Tiger needed help finding an opening to the attic and "meowed" at the mouse, who thought, "Haha, you can't get to me."

Little David heard Tiger meowing and went to check on him. "Tiger, what's wrong?" David asked.

"Oh, Tiger, it's only a mouse! He won't hurt you. Please leave him alone."

Tiger refused to leave him alone until he emerged from the attic.

When David calls Tiger to eat, the mouse finally thinks he is free. That big orange cat had left.

The mouse decided to come down from the attic to search for food.

Tiger caught a whiff of the mouse and dashed after it. David called out, "Stop, Tiger! Don't harm him." Mom started shouting, "Tiger, go get him!" David intervened, "No, Mom, he isn't hurting anyone."

"David, he will get into all our food;
you can't have him as a pet," Mom
said.

"I will feed Bell. I promise he will not eat our food," Mom laughed. "So, you named him already! Oh, son, what am I going to do with you?"

Mom said, "Okay, David, the first time he gets into the cabinets to eat our food, I will let Tiger get him."

Tiger is eager to play with the mouse, but David refuses to let him play.

So, Tiger would watch Bell, hoping he would get into the food, but he never did.

David believes this mouse is unlike
a typical house mouse; he seems
too intelligent.

While Tiger was climbing his playset, he looked up and saw Bell. For the first time, he wanted to watch Bell play rather than use him as a toy.

Dad walked into the living room and remarked, "David, it seems like Tiger and Bell are starting to get along."

Bell and Tiger started playing together.

Later, David went to his room to get a book and noticed the cat and mouse sleeping in Tiger's bed. He started laughing. "What an odd pair," he thought.

The next day, David went to school and told his friend Barney about his cat and mouse. Barney asked, "Can I come over to see them?" David replied, "Sure, come on over."

Barney came over on Saturday to meet Tiger and Bell. At first, he was a little scared of the mouse but realized Bell was harmless.

David's Mom said, "I just made a batch of cookies fresh from the oven, boys. Would you like some with milk?" They both replied in unison, "Yes, please."

After the boys ate their cookies, Mom announced, "Barney's Mom called and said it was time for him to go home." Barney said, "Thank you for inviting me to meet Tiger and Bell; it was fun." David replied, "Come back again; I had fun also."

Mom asked, "Did you and Barney have a good time today?" David replied, "Tiger and Bell had as much fun as we did, especially eating the cookies." Mom laughed and said, "You should have Barney come over again soon and maybe invite some of your other friends too." David said, "That would be fun; thanks, Mom."